scrapworking 2

Scrapworks believes that scrapbooking and paper crafting should be fun and simple enough that anyone can achieve a polished look when crafting their projects. This is why Scrapworks is committed to providing paper crafters with products that are uncomplicated, color coordinated, and safe to use with precious memorabilia.

Scrapworking 2 is the second book in a series containing ideas that can be easily adapted by crafters with any level of experience. As you study its pages, you will realize that *Scrapworking 2* has become one of your most important sources of inspiration. You'll appreciate the fact that embellishments included in these projects serve to focus the viewer's attention on photographs, titles, and thoughtful journal entries without overwhelming the eye with unnecessary trivia.

So let's get started. Grab some pictures, your craft supplies, and let the *Scrapworking* begin!

contributors

Denise Hoogland and her best friend, Sarah Goodman, co-founded Scrapworks a little over a year ago. Other than scrapbooking, Denise enjoys shopping and hanging out with family and friends. She enjoys graphic design, as well as conceiving innovative new products to share with inspired paper crafters all over the world. She loves working along side the innovative Scrapworks design team and is truly amazed at the depth of creativity they exhibit as they come up with new ideas. Denise and the love of her life, her husband CJ, recently moved to Salt Lake City, Utah, along with their very energetic children (Jayden – 5, Madi – 4, and Abbey – 3).

Jackie Bonnette is a stay-at-home mother of three who lives on a farm and ranch in Taber, Alberta, Canada with her husband, Bernie. Jackie began scrapbooking almost five years ago as a creative means of recording her family's everyday life, moments and memories – but it has become so much more to her now. At the end of a day filled with caring for her three busy little people, she has found that a few hours spent scrapping in the quiet of the evening (or even far into the wee hours) have become a type of therapy that helps her to remain sane.

Jackie loves all aspects of the craft: the creative energy it allows her to spend, getting together with friends to scrapbook (or to just share ideas), and expeditions to gather supplies. Most of Jackie's materials make their way to her from the great scrapbooking source, www.twopeasinabucket.com, where Jackie is fortunate enough to be a designer.

Jamie Waters currently lives in South Pasadena, California with her husband, Chris, and their three children (Kira – 8, Cameron – 5, and Caleb – 3). She is a stay-at-home mother who is always on the go, so it's not surprising to hear what a fun outlet scrapbooking is for her. Jamie enjoys every step of the creative process – from taking numerous photographs to choosing the cardstock she will use for her layouts. Most of all, she loves to use scrapbooking as a means of documenting life's small, but important moments, such as the little sparks she witnesses each day in her children or the small special moments that will soon pass her by.

When Jamie is not busy managing school schedules, she enjoys watching good movies and going out to dinner. Ever looking towards the future, Jamie states that she is looking forward to traveling with her children as they get older.

Shelley Sullivan

Kim Heffington has been involved in scrapbooking for six years. She feels that her photographs should be the most important elements on her pages: strong photos make great scrapbook layouts! Although Kim has always had an interest in photography, it wasn't until she began scrapbooking that her interest evolved into a passion. Kim currently owns her own photography studio in Arizona, where she lives with her husband and two children.

Shelley Sullivan began scrapbooking six years ago, but didn't really find her "groove" until she switched from 12" x 12" to 8.5" x 11" layouts two years ago. She loves this hobby because it provides a creative outlet that gives her a way to craft a legacy of love for her daughter, Chandler. Shelley views scrapbooking layouts as not only a way to document events, but also as a vehicle to record affirmations and advice that she wants to pass down through the generations. Shelley was inducted into the 2002 Creative Keepsakes Hall of Fame and is also a part of the Creating Garden design team at www.twopeasinabucket.com.

Stacey Sattler is an elementary school art teacher who loves to learn, create, and share. She lives in Ohio with her husband, Jason, and their two sons – Carter and Riley. Stacey became wild about scrapbooking after diving headfirst into the craft in 1998. She loves taking photographs and using those "perfect" shots (and the not-so-perfect ones) to tell the story of her family. She is passionate about capturing the "everyday" moments, the silly expressions, and the precious faces that make up her world. Placing her photos on a layout she has created by combining paper, accents, and journal entries is very satisfying and fun for this inspired artist.

Alphadotz™ Facts

Scrapworks Alphadotz are great little alphabet letters or word punch outs that are printed on heavy cardstock. They have been designed to coordinate perfectly with Scrapworks Hugz™. Alphadotz can also be used without Hugz by sticking them to your project with a little adhesive.

Snow Day 2003
materials
Scrapworks Baby Doll (Jig Jag – plain side) paper
Scrapworks Alphadotz
Scrapworks Hugz
Scrapworks Waxy Flax
Bazzill Basics cardstock

by Denise Hoogland

Spring Things
materials
Scrapworks Baby Doll (Fat Stripes) paper
Scrapworks Cool Boy (Fat Stripes) paper
Scrapworks Alphadotz
Scrapworks Hugz
Scrapworks Waxy Flax
Savvy Stamps image stamps
PSX letter stamps
Hero Arts letter stamps
Me & My Big Ideas letter stickers

by Jackie Bonette

Birthday Boy

materials
Scrapworks Alphadotz
Scrapworks Spiral Clips
unknown: cardstock

by Jamie Waters

You

materials
Scrapworks Cool Boy (Fat
Stripes) paper
Scrapworks Alphadotz

by Kim Heffington

Alphadotz™ Tips

Alphadotz have been designed to fit perfectly inside Scrapworks simple-to-use Hugz™. Placing them on your project is as easy as 1-2-3!

1. Slip the Alphadotz into the Hugz.

2. Press the prongs of the Hugz through your paper. It's effortless as can be if you use your Scrapworks Pushpad™ while you work.

3. Bend the prongs down (the end of a pen or pencil works great for this) and you are finished.

Brothers

materials
Scrapworks Cool Boy (Low Down) paper
Scrapworks Cool Boy (Squiggle Worm – plain side) paper
Scrapworks Alphadotz
Scrapworks Looking Glass Frames
Scrapworks Studs

by Jamie Waters

Abbey

materials
Scrapworks Alphadotz
unknown: cardstock

by Denise Hoogland

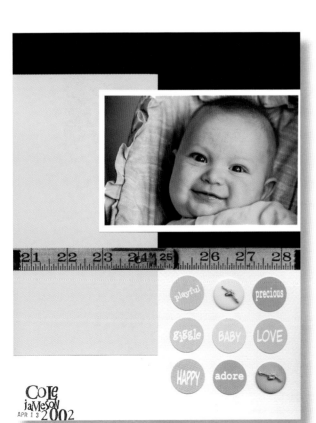

Cole Jameson

materials
Scrapworks Baby Doll (Squiggle
Worm – plain side) paper
Scrapworks Alphadotz
Making Memories buttons
Rebecca Sower's Nostalgiques stickers
PSX letter stamps
Hero Arts letter stamps
All Night Media stamps
unknown: cardstock

by Jackie Bonette

Alphadotz™ Tips

Here are some fun ways to use Alphadotz to add interest to your layout title:

• Vary the colors of Alphadotz you use within the same title or word
• Use cardstock and metal Alphadotz together in the same word or title
• Vary the use of Hugz™ within the same word or title
• Combine single letter Alphadotz with word Alphadotz in the same title

A Little Brighter

materials
Scrapworks Super Hero (Low Down) paper
Scrapworks Alphadotz
Scrapworks Hugz
Paper House Productions stickers
PSX letter stamps
Hero Arts letter stamps
unknown: cardstock

by Jackie Bonette

Joy

materials
Scrapworks Super Hero (Low Down) paper
Scrapworks Alphadotz
Scrapworks Hugz
unknown: cardstock

by Jamie Waters

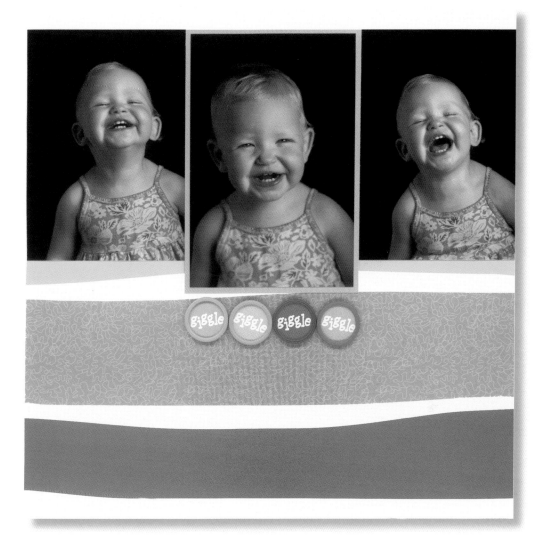

Giggle

materials
Scrapworks Super Hero (Fat Stripes) paper
Scrapworks Alphadotz
Scrapworks Hugz

by Kim Heffington

Alphadotz™ Tips

Here are some fun ways to embellish your pages with Alphadotz:

• Alphadotz can be used as charms! Just punch tiny holes in them and string them onto your project with Waxy Flax™ or fiber. Put jump rings through the holes you have punched before stringing them if you would like them to dangle freely.

• Attach Alphadotz to a ribbon and string the ribbon across your page to make a border with a message.

• Using a strip of vellum, sew small pockets - leaving the top edge open. Slip Alphadotz into the pockets.

Abbey

`materials`
Scrapworks Baby Doll (Super Funk) paper
Scrapworks Baby Doll (Jig Jag) paper
Scrapworks Baby Doll (Fat Stripes) paper
Scrapworks Baby Doll (Low Down) paper
Scrapworks Baby Doll (Squiggle Worm) paper
Scrapworks Baby Doll (Original Stripes) paper
Scrapworks Alphadotz
Scrapworks Hugz

by Denise Hoogland

2 Brothers

materials
Scrapworks Cool Boy (Super Funk) paper
Scrapworks Cool Boy (Fat Stripes – plain side) paper
Scrapworks Alphadotz
Scrapworks Hugz
Sonnets sticker
PSX letter stamps
Hero Arts letter stamps
Lost Art Treasures mini brads
Two Peas in a Bucket metal tag
unknown: cardstock

by Jackie Bonette

Fresh Cut

materials
Scrapworks Cool Boy (Super Funk) paper
Scrapworks Alphadotz
Scrapworks Hugz
Making Memories Simply Stated rub-ons
unknown: cardstock

by Kim Heffington

Metal Alphadotz™ Facts

Metal Alphadotz are lightweight, thin metal discs that allow you to effortlessly add the popular metallic embellishment look to your layouts. Fix them to your project by adding just a small touch of glue to the back of the disc. However, if you use them in combination with Scrapworks round Hugz™, you don't even have to use adhesives to add them to your page!

Jayden and Chandler

materials

Scrapworks Super Hero (Super Funk) paper
Scrapworks Super Hero (Fat Stripes – plain side) paper
Scrapworks Metal Alphadotz
Scrapworks Studs

by Denise Hoogland

Fall Day

materials
Scrapworks Cool Boy (Fat Stripes
– plain side) paper
Scrapworks Cool Boy (Low Down
– plain side) paper
Scrapworks Cool Boy (Jig Jag
– plain side) paper
Scrapworks Metal Alphadotz
Scrapworks Hugz
Scrapworks Waxy Flax
unknown: vellum

by Denise Hoogland

FALL DAYS...
- cotton candy
- carmel apples
- **pumpkin pie**
  and
- hay rides

One Hot Day

materials
Scrapworks Super Hero (Super
Funk) paper
Scrapworks Metal Alphadotz
Scrapworks Hugz
unknown: cardstock

by Jamie Waters

Metal Alphadotz™ Tips

Use Metal Alphadotz to add interest to your layout title in the following ways:
• Spell out only the main word in your title with Metal Alphadotz
• Use a contrasting color behind the Metal Alphadotz to make your title pop
• Mix and match them in the same word with cardstock Alphadotz or letter stickers
• Use more than one contrasting color of cardstock behind letters in the same word
• Use a tiny pop dot foam sticker behind each Metal Alphadotz to add depth

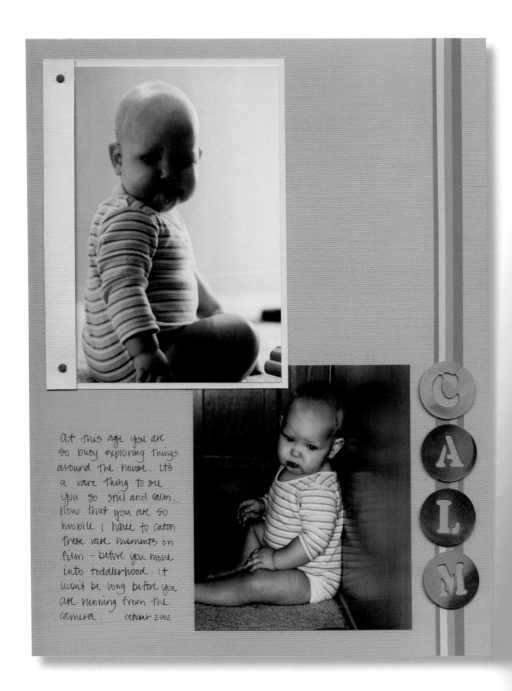

Calm

materials
Scrapworks Hot Girl (Low Down) paper
Scrapworks Metal Alphadotz
Scrapworks Studs
Bazzill Basics cardstock

by Kim Heffington

Madi

materials
Scrapworks Hot Girl (Jig Jag – plain side) paper
Scrapworks Super Hero (Fat Stripes – plain side) paper
Scrapworks Metal Alphadotz
Scrapworks I lugz
Scrapworks Waxy Fax
Making Memories Simply Stated rub-ons

by Denise Hoogland

Hugz™ Facts

Hugz are great little colored metal circles and square frames that have prongs on the back of them, allowing you to attach them to your project without pre-punching holes or using tools. Available in a large variety of sizes and colors, you can find just the right one to match your layout. They are perfect for easily giving your title that polished look that you love!

Stroller Smitten

materials
Scrapworks Cool Boy (Jig Jag) paper
Scrapworks Baby Doll (Super Funk) paper
Scrapworks Baby Doll (Original Stripes – plain side) paper
Scrapworks Alphadotz
Scrapworks Hugz
Scrapworks Studs
Sue Dreamer letter stickers
Stampin' Up! ink

by Kim Heffington

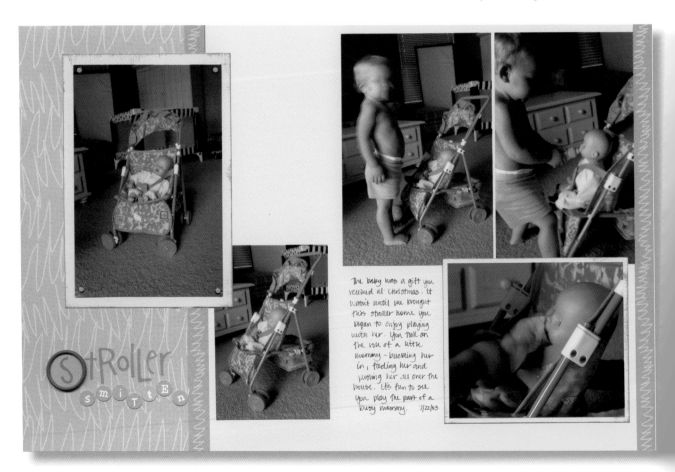

Go Fish

materials
Scrapworks Cool Boy (Super Funk) paper
Scrapworks Hugz
Doodle Bug letter stickers
unknown: letter stamps and cardstock

by Shelley Sullivan

Tips for Hugz ™

Here are a few ways to use Hugz to add interest to your layout title:
• Use them with Scrapworks Alph-adotz™ to frame a single letter or a single word
• Use them to frame letter stickers
• Use them to accent shapes or designs (Example: creating the center of a flower)

Don't forget to use your Scrap-works Pushpad™ to make setting Hugz a breeze!

Groovy 60's Girl

materials
Scrapworks Hot Girl (Squiggle Worm – plain side) paper
Scrapworks Hot Girl (Original Stripe – plain side) paper
Scrapworks Hugz
Educational Insights letter stamps

by Shelley Sullivan

Failure is Impossible

materials
Scrapworks Baby Doll (Squiggle
Worm – plain side) paper
Scrapworks Baby Doll (Jig Jag
– plain side) paper
Scrapworks Hugz
Provo Craft Collage Pad handmade
paper
Colorbox ink
unknown: cardstock

by Shelley Sullivan

Country Girl

materials
Scrapworks Hot Girl (Super Funk) paper
Scrapworks Hot Girl (Jig Jag) paper
Scrapworks Hot Girl (Squiggle Worm) paper
Scrapworks Super Hero (Jig Jag – plain side) paper
Scrapworks Hugz
Scrapworks Studs
Making Memories Magnetic Date Stamp
Two Peas in a Bucket Fairy Princess font
unknown: cardstock

by Jackie Bonette

Summer 2001

Clips Facts

Scrapworks Clips are available in several bright colors and shapes and are large enough to stand alone as decorative accents on your project. Clips are trouble-free to use. Just slip the frame of the clip behind a paper edge in the same way you use a metal bookmark when reading your favorite novel. What could be simpler?

My Joy

materials
Scrapworks Baby Doll (Fat Stripes) paper
Scrapworks Baby Doll (Low Down) paper
Scrapworks Baby Doll (Jig Jag – plain side) paper
Scrapworks Alphadotz
Scrapworks Spiral Clips
PSX letter stamps
Hero Arts letter stamps
Carbonated and Gothic fonts

by Jackie Bonette

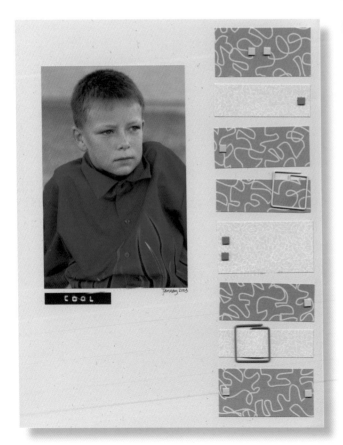

Cool

materials
Scrapworks Cool Boy (Squiggle Worm) paper
Scrapworks Cool Boy (Fat Stripes) paper
Scrapworks Square Clips
Scrapworks Studs
P.Real Life stickers
unknown: cardstock

by Kim Heffington

Dream

materials
Scrapworks Hot Girl (Fat Stripes) paper
Scrapworks Alphadotz
Scrapworks Spiral Clip
Scrapworks Waxy Flax
unknown: cardstock

by Jamie Waters

How Cute Are You?

materials
Scrapworks Super Hero (Original Stripes – plain side) paper
Scrapworks Super Hero (Jig Jag – plain side) paper
Scrapworks Baby Doll (Jig Jag – plain side) paper
Scrapworks Square Clips
Savvy Stamps paper flowers
PSX letter stamps
unknown: jewelry tags, small jewels, letter stickers, cardstock

by Shelley Sullivan

Clips Tips

Fun ways to include Clips on your project include:
• Use them to attach a photo or a journaling block to your page
• Use them to hold a small accent such as a title, subtitle, photo or tag
• Thread a strip of cardstock through a square-edged clip to create the effect of a belt buckle
• Use an Alpha Clip to highlight an important letter in your title
• Clip them to a vellum pocket. This allows all of the edges of the clip to be seen
• Thread a bead or jewel through one end of the clip for a special accent

Riley and Papa

materials
Scrapworks Cool Boy (Super Funk) paper
Scrapworks Heart Clip
Scrapworks Slide Frame
PSX letter stamps
Hero Arts letter stamps
Colorbox ink
unknown: cardstock

by Stacey Sattler

Play Hard

materials
Scrapworks Cool Boy (Low Down) paper
Scrapworks Super Hero (Squiggle Worm – plain side) paper
Scrapworks Alphadotz
Scrapworks Alpha Clip
Scrapworks Alphabet Stud
unknown: cardstock

by Jackie Bonette

Magic

materials
Scrapworks Super Hero (Squiggle Worm – plain side) paper
Scrapworks Super Hero (Original Stripes – plain side) paper
Scrapworks Cool Boy (Fat Stripes – plain side) paper
Scrapworks Spiral Clip
Scrapworks Studs
Making Memories Simply Stated rub-on
unknown: cardstock

by Jamie Waters

Clips Tips

Fresh ways to attach Clips to your layout include:
• Use a little adhesive to attach it so that the entire clip is exposed
• String the clip onto Waxy Flax, fiber, or ribbon. Attach to your layout to create an exciting page border
• Use fiber or thread to sew one edge of the clip to the paper
• Use jump rings to hang the clip from a ribbon or fiber
• Tie ribbon to one side of the clip. Sew the ribbon down, leaving just a small amount free, which will give the appearance that the clip is dangling.

Conversations

materials
Scrapworks Super Hero (Low Down) paper
Scrapworks Alpha Clip
unknown: cardstock

by Shelley Sullivan

Conversations with you are so important to me. You've got the gift of gab and you bestow it on me often. I love that! I hope you'll always gab freely with me. ☺

Smelling The Daisies

materials
Scrapworks Flower Alpha Clip
Scrapworks Studs
SEI letter stickers
unknown: vellum and cardstock

by Denise Hoogland

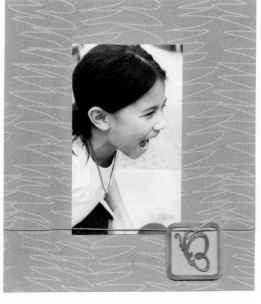

Sweet Laughter

materials
Scrapworks Hot Girl (Jig Jag) paper
Scrapworks Alphadotz
Scrapworks Butterfly Clip
Scrapworks Studs
Scrapworks Waxy Flax
unknown: cardstock

by Jamie Waters

Frames Facts

Scrapworks Metal Frames have prongs on the back of them to allow you to attach them to your project without adhesives. Here are the easy steps you follow to set them: Locate the spot on your project in which you would like to attach the frame. Push the prongs through the paper. Bend the prongs flat and your frame is set.

Plastic Scrapworks Slide Frames or Looking Glass Frames (which are hollow clear bubbles that you can fill with embellishments like sand, beads, or sea shells) must be set with adhesive. Trace a thin pencil line on your paper around the frame you wish to set. Next, trace a thin line of clear adhesive (like Diamond Glaze) on the pencil stroke and press your frame into place.

Original

materials
Scrapworks Baby Doll (Low Down) paper
Scrapworks Baby Doll (Fat Stripes – plain side) paper
Scrapworks Concho
Scrapworks Slide Frame
PSX letter stamps
Hero Arts letter stamps
Catslife Press image stamps
Me & My Big Ideas letter stickers
Doodle Bug letter stickers
unknown: cardstock

by Jackie Bonette

You Love Me

materials
Scrapworks Baby Doll (Jig Jag – plain side) paper
Scrapworks Alphadotz
Scrapworks Slide Frames
Acoustic Bass font
Flower Design: Scrapworks' product packaging
unknown: cardstock

by Shelley Sullivan

Creative

materials
Scrapworks Baby Doll (Low Down) paper
Scrapworks Cool Boy (Fat Stripes) paper
Scrapworks Alphadotz
Scrapworks Studs
Scrapworks Frame
PSX letter stamps
unknown: cardstock

by Jackie Bonette

scrapworking

Frames Tips

Scrapworks Frames have endless possibilities. Here are a few that you might want to try:
• Give titles that little extra pop by framing the main word
• Use them to frame stickers, designs or images
• Back the frame with printed or plain contrasting paper
• Frame a few important words in your journal entry
• Frame an important detail in your photograph
• Create a shaker box. Cover the top of the frame with a piece of clear transparency. Fill the opening with small, flat memorabilia. Glue the back of the frame to your layout.

Cozy

materials
Scrapworks Baby Doll (Jig Jag) paper
Scrapworks Cool Boy (Fat Stripes – plain side) paper
Scrapworks Alphadotz
Scrapworks Frame
Scrapworks Button Studs
Two Peas in a Bucket Rickety font
unknown: cardstock

by Jamie Waters

Sweet

materials
Scrapworks Baby Doll (Squiggle Worm) paper
Scrapworks Super Hero (Super Funk) paper
Scrapworks Super Hero (Squiggle Worm – plain side) paper
Scrapworks Looking Glass Frame
EK Success Jolee's flowers
Li'l Davis Alpha Pebbles
unknown: cardstock

by Jamie Waters

Play

materials
Scrapworks Baby Doll (Fat Stripes)
Scrapworks Alphadotz
Scrapworks Plain Frame

by Kim Heffington

Thanksgiving day in aunt Deb's backyard   11/2002

Studs Tips

Studs are colored metal embellishments that attach to your project through Scrapworks easy-to-use prong technology. They are available in a large variety of shapes, sizes, and colors. When piercing your paper with the prongs of a stud, make sure to use the Scrapworks Pushpad™. It has been designed to help reduce the pressure on the paper as the prongs pierce through it so that no crumpling or unsightly marks appear on your project.

Pout

materials
Scrapworks Super Hero (Low Down) paper
Scrapworks Hot Girl (Jig Jag – plain side)
Scrapworks Hugz
Scrapworks Metal Alphabet Studs

by Stacey Sattler

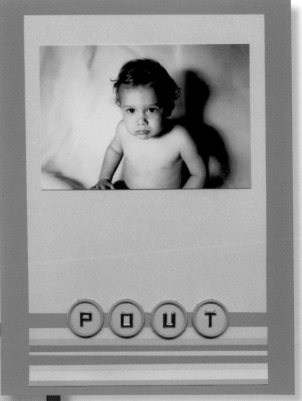

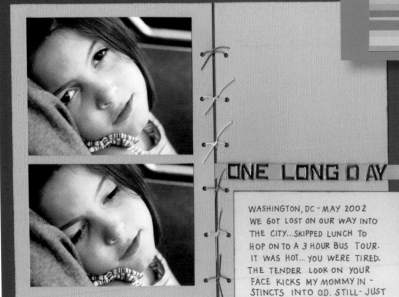

ONE LONG DAY

WASHINGTON, DC - MAY 2002
WE GOT LOST ON OUR WAY INTO
THE CITY...SKIPPED LUNCH TO
HOP ON TO A 3 HOUR BUS TOUR.
IT WAS HOT.. YOU WERE TIRED.
THE TENDER LOOK ON YOUR
FACE KICKS MY MOMMY IN-
STINCTS INTO O.D. STILL- JUST
SEEING THESE PHOTOS.

One Long Day

materials
Scrapworks Cool Boy (Squiggle Worm – plain side) paper
Scrapworks Waxy Flax
Scrapworks Alphabet Studs
Nick Bantok ink
unknown: cardstock

by Shelley Sullivan

Skater

materials
Scrapworks Super Hero (Low Down) paper
Scrapworks Super Hero (Original Stripes – plain side)
Scrapworks Alphabet Studs
Scrapworks Studs
unknown: cardstock

by Kim Heffington

Studs Tips

Studs are so versatile. Here are a few fun ways to use them to add interest to your layout:
• Use Studs to attach photos, tags, word strips, contrasting paper or other embellishments to your project
• Create titles with Alphabet Studs
• Add small spots of color interest to your project with Studs
• Use a single Alphabet Stud to highlight an important letter in your title or journaling block
• Hang a tag from a Stud by threading a piece of Waxy Flax or other fiber through a hole you have punched in the tag. Tie the other end of the fiber around the Stud to finish.

26 Words

materials
Scrapworks Hot Girl (Squiggle Worm and Super Funk – plain side) paper
Scrapworks Baby Doll (Jig Jag and Low Down – plain side) paper
Scrapworks Cool Boy (Squiggle Worm and Jig Jag – plain side) paper
Scrapworks Studs
PSX letter stamps
Rubber City letter stamps
Stamp Works letter stamps
Educational Insights letter stamps
Oh Sandra, Dingos, Emma Script fonts
Colorbox ink
unknown: cardstock

by Shelley Sullivan

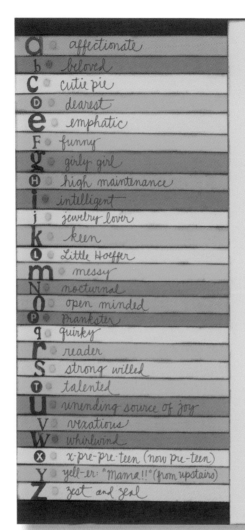

a • affectionate
b • beloved
C • cutie pie
D • dearest
e • emphatic
F • funny
g • girly girl
H • high maintenance
• intelligent
j • jewelry lover
k • keen
L • Little Hoeffer
m • messy
N • nocturnal
O • open minded
P • prankster
q • quirky
r • reader
S • strong willed
T • talented
U • unending source of joy
V • vexatious
W • whirlwind
X • x-pre-pre-teen (now pre-teen)
Y • yell-er: "Mama!!" (from upstairs)
Z • zest and zeal

26words are not enough to describe all that you are.

Farewell to
FOUR

My boy is on the brink of a new year.
Year four was fun.
New school, new friends,
now he will welcome new adventures.

November 2003

Wonder

materials
Scrapworks Hot Girl (Squiggle
Worm) paper
Scrapworks Studs
Bazzill Basics cardstock
Century Gothic and Avalon fonts

by Kim Heffington

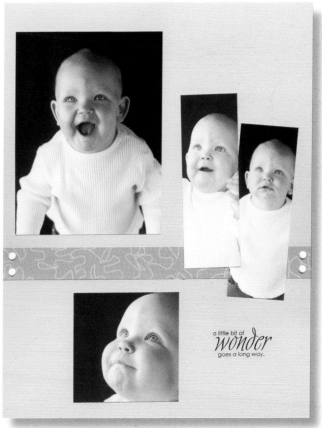

a little bit of
wonder
goes a long way.

Farewell To Four

materials
Scrapworks Studs
Bazzill Basics cardstock
Stone Sans font

by Jamie Waters

Waxy Flax ™ Facts

Waxy Flax is a wax coated thread that stays put once you have molded it into any shape that you wish! It is available in a large variety of colors, making it possible for you to find just the right hue to match your layout. Adding stitched embellishments to your projects is simple with Waxy Flax, as the threads are durable enough to be stitched through your cardstock without shredding or falling apart.

.

Chandler Elora

materials

Scrapworks Hot Girl (Squiggle Worm – plain side) paper
Scrapworks Cool Boy (Fat Stripes – plain side) paper
Scrapworks Waxy Flax
Dearest Swash font
unknown: cardstock

by Shelley Sullivan

Brother - Sister

materials
Scrapworks Cool Boy (Squiggle Worm) paper
Scrapworks Alphadotz
Scrapworks Studs
Scrapworks Waxy Flax

by Denise Hoogland

Smile

materials
Scrapworks Super Hero (Jig Jag – plain side) paper
Scrapworks Super Hero (Original Stripes) paper
Scrapworks Alphadotz
Scrapworks Spiral Clip
Scrapworks Waxy Flax
PSX letter stamps
Hero Arts letter stamps

by Stacey Sattler

Waxy Flax™ Tips

Need some ideas for using Scrapworks Waxy Flax™ on your projects? Here's just a few:

• Mold Waxy Flax into words, designs or shapes. If you wish, use a tiny touch of glue or a few Scrapworks Studs to help set the shape permanently to your project.

• Tie Waxy Flax bows around a strip of contrasting cardstock to create simple, but elegant embellishments

• Stitch tags, word strips, or contrasting blocks of cardstock to your project with Waxy Flax

• Tie multiple coordinating or contrasting pieces of Waxy Flax through holes punched in the ends of tags

• Use pieces of Waxy Flax to create borders or emphasis blocks on your layouts

Joy

materials
Scrapworks Baby Doll (Low Down – plain side) paper
Scrapworks Baby Doll (Jig Jag – plain side) paper
Scrapworks Baby Doll (Squiggle Worm – plain side) paper
Scrapworks Waxy Flax
Colorbox ink
unknown: cardstock

by Shelley Sullivan

Precious

materials
Scrapworks Hot Girl (Squiggle
Worm) paper
Scrapworks Waxy Flax
Scrapworks Studs
Making Memories Simply
Stated rub-ons
Family Treasures punch
unknown: cardstock

by Kim Heffington

Cards Tips

Nothing declares that you care more than when you give someone a hand-made card, and what fun they are to make! Scrapworks products are perfectly suited for card making, because their bright colors and cheerful appearance makes you feel good when you look at them. The clean lines adapt well to any style, from whimsical to classy. You are only limited by your imagination. But don't worry; if you don't feel particularly creative, just use one of the great projects in this section to get you jump started!

Thinking of You

materials
Scrapworks Cool Boy (Super Funk) paper
Scrapworks Studs
Colorbox ink
PSX stamps

by Shelley Sullivan

Congratulations

materials
Scrapworks Cool Boy (Super Funk) paper
Scrapworks Cool Boy (Fat Stripes – plain side) paper
Scrapworks Frame
Scrapworks Button Stud
Scrapworks Safety Pin Stud

by Jamie Waters

All Occasion Card Set

materials
Scrapworks Cool Boy (Low Down) paper
Scrapworks Alphadotz
Ranger ink
unknown: cardstock

by Stacey Sattler

Celebrate

materials
Scrapworks Alphadotz
Scrapworks Studs
unknown: cardstock

by Jamie Waters

Thanks A Bunch

materials
Scrapworks Super Hero (Jig Jag) paper
Scrapworks Alphadotz
Scrapworks Hugz
O'Scrap flower stickers

by Denise Hoogland

Cards Tips

Looking for ideas for making your cards unique? Here are just a few to begin with:

• Use Scrapworks Alphadotz™ (with or without Hugz™) or Alphabet Studs to create your card's message

• Use stickers, stamps, rub-ons or hand-lettering to create your card's message

• Print your card's message using computer fonts. Use a Hugz or a Scrapworks Frame to emphasize the important words

• Back your message with a piece of coordinating or contrasting paper to bring emphasis to your message

• Frame a Scrapworks Spiral Clip with a contrasting color Hugz to create a unique embellishment

Sparkle

materials
Scrapworks Baby Doll (Jig Jag) paper
Scrapworks Baby Doll (Original Stripe – plain side) paper
Scrapworks Metal Alphadotz
Scrapworks Hugz
Scrapworks Studs
Making Memories Simply Stated rub-ons

by Denise Hoogland

Missing U

materials
Scrapworks Alphadotz
Colorbox ink
PSX ink
unknown: cardstock

by Shelley Sullivan

You Are One Cool Cat!

materials
Scrapworks Baby Doll (Squiggle
Worm – plain side) paper
Scrapworks Hugz
Hallmark cat stickers
Colorbox ink
Hootie font
unknown: cardstock

by Shelley Sullivan

Love You

materials
Scrapworks Cool Boy (Original
Stripe) paper
Scrapworks Hot Girl (Fat Stripes
– plain side) paper
Scrapworks Metal Alphadotz
Colorbox ink
Offray ribbon
unknown: cardstock

by Shelley Sullivan

Cards Tips

Here are some innovative ways to create unique homemade envelopes and tags:

• Use Scrapworks double-sided paper (it is printed on one side and plain on the other) to create coordinated cards and envelopes

• Need a great pattern to create an envelope? Look through your pre-made envelopes to find a size and style that you like. Carefully take it apart to create a pattern, altering the details in any way that you like. What inexpensive fun!

• Trace your favorite tag as a pattern that can be used in the future

• Use a Scrapworks Hugz™ to support the edge of a tag hole. Then your ribbon won't rip out when tugged!

Love U

materials
Scrapworks Hot Girl (Jig Jag) paper
Scrapworks Hot Girl (Original Stripes) paper
Scrapworks Hot Girl (Squiggle Worm – plain side) paper
Scrapworks Baby Girl (Original Stripe – plain side) paper
Scrapworks Hugz

by Kim Heffington

Happy Birthday

materials
Scrapworks Hot Girl (Squiggle Worm – plain side) paper
Scrapworks Stud
Scrapworks Waxy Flax
Bazzill Basics cardstock
unknown: chipboard and paper

by Shelley Sullivan

Girlie

materials
Scrapworks Baby Doll (Fat Stripes) paper
Scrapworks Studs
Scrapworks Waxy Flax
Scrapworks Hugz
Scrapworks Frame
Making Memories metal letters
unknown: ribbon

by Stacey Sattler

Carter and Riley

materials
Scrapworks Super Hero (Super Funk) paper
Scrapworks Metal Alphadotz
Scrapworks Studs
PSX letter stamps
Staz-On ink
unknown: ribbon, small jewelry tag, round metal rimmed tags

by Stacey Sattler

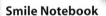

Glen Lake

materials
Scrapworks Baby Doll (Super Funk) paper
Scrapworks Alphadotz
Scrapworks Hugz
Ma Sexy font
unknown: small envelope and fabric

by Stacey Sattler

Smile Notebook

materials
Scrapworks Super Hero (Fat Stripes – plain side) paper
Scrapworks Cool Boy (Fat Stripes – plain side) paper
Scrapworks Baby Doll (Jig Jag – plain side) paper
Scrapworks Cool Boy (Super Funk – plain side) paper
Scrapworks Hugz
Scrapworks Spiral Clips
Bazzill Basics cardstock

by Stacey Sattler

We want to give a great big thanks and "Hugz" to all of the contributers of *Scrapworking 2*. Their talent is awesome and is only shadowed by their great spirits and willingness to share their gifts and memories with the world. Kudos to you all!

about scrapworks

Scrapworks was formed with the vision of helping ordinary people discover their creative side while preserving their memories. Our goal is to produce products and publications that will help crafters find inspiration to create their own unique projects. *Scrapworking 2* is the second in a series of books that will help crafters learn useful techniques to use when making their own paper projects.

Scrapworking 2
Published by
Scrapworks
3038 Specialty Circle, Suite C
Salt Lake City, Utah 84115
www.scrapworks.com

Scrapworking 2 is the second book in a series published by Scrapworks.

Publisher: Scrapworks
Book Design: Denise Hoogland
Cover Design: Denise Hoogland
Creative Director: Denise Hoogland
Idea Book Coordinator: Shelley Sullivan
Writers: Rozanne Paxman and *Scrapworking 2* design team
Editor: Rozanne Paxman

For information about bulk sales or promotional pricing, please contact us at scrapworking2@scrapworks.com or call 1-801-363-1010.

ISBN 0-9749192-0-9

Printed in the USA